God Alone and I

Carmelite Meditations

Compiled and adapted
by the
Carmel of Flemington

To our devoted members
of the
Secular Order
of Discalced Carmelites
for whom this book
was compiled.

Nihil Obstat

William A. Margerum, S.T.D.

Imprimatur

✠George W. Ahr, S.T.D.
Bishop of Trenton
April 15, 1965

ISBN: 978-0-9829717-1-0

Table of Contents

God Alone and I

THE INVITATION OF GRACE

"Christ does not force our wills. He will only take what we give Him, but He will never give Himself entirely to us until we give ourselves entirely to Him."

(St. Teresa of Jesus)

Our Lord told us that He would always come and stand at the threshold but it is the soul that must open the door. "Behold, I stand at the door and knock; if any man ... open to Me the door, I will come in." Yes, He will come over and over again until the hour of our death and only the soul can put a stop to His coming. These knockings are inspirations of grace, silent and secret. We are free to accept them or reject them. Our Lord will never force our will, but if we correspond to these inspirations with great fidelity, He will enter in and take possession of our souls. Then, little by little, His light and truth will enlighten every hour of our life. Often we are held back by the secret fear that "having Him, we may have naught beside." For years, St. Teresa could not find the courage to give up certain infidelities until one day she knelt before an image of Our Lord being scourged, and begged Him to take away from her the power to resist Him. She said, "I then made greater progress; for I was now very distrustful of myself and placed all my confidence in God."

Colloquy

"O my Lord, the fault is not Yours that those who love You do not do great things, but in our cowardice and littleness of mind! How we never make good resolutions without being filled with a thousand fears and considerations of human prudence! O how good a friend You are, O my Lord! How you comfort and endure, and wait for souls to make themselves like unto You!"

(St. Teresa of Jesus)

❧❧❧ PRAYER ❦❦❦

"Prayer is the door to great graces. If this door be shut, I do not see how God can bestow them."

(St. Teresa of Jesus)

Our Lord said, "Pray always." He was not speaking only to a few disciples, but to every Christian throughout the ages, and He never commands the impossible. As members of the Secular Order of Discalced Carmelites, He will give us the special graces we need to fulfill this precept, for our vocation is to be persons of prayer living in the world. In spite of all the distractions in my state of life, I must firmly believe that I can pray always — not trusting in my own power, for I have none, but fully confident in the power and mercy of our Lord.

In what does "praying always" consist? St. Teresa, our spiritual Mother, said that prayer is a loving conversation between the soul and God, "Whom we know loves us." This loving colloquy can be carried on during the day, even at the times I am working, at home with my family, or going to a party. I only need to turn my soul to God Who is within me, and unite my actions to His holy will, telling Him that I do them for love of Him and with Him. Then all my actions, my whole day, become a continual prayer. With St. Teresa, "Let us beseech God to give us the grace and resolution to strive for this blessing with all our might."

Colloquy

"O Lord, let me live with You as with a friend! Wherever I am or whatever I do, You never leave me alone; grant that I, too, may always remain with You. At every hour of the day and night, in joy or sorrow, in every work and action, may I always know how to find You within me. Let me remain in You, to offer myself to others through You, to attend to all my duties, while always penetrating further into Your divine depths."

(Bl. Elizabeth of the Trinity)

✎✎✎ ST. JOSEPH ✐✐✐

"Those who are devoted to prayer should, in a special manner, cherish devotion to St. Joseph."

(St. Teresa of Jesus)

The Carmelites have always looked upon St. Joseph as a tender and loving father, and a special patron of the interior life. St. Teresa said, "Let him who cannot find anyone to teach him to pray, choose this glorious Saint for his master, and he will not stray from the right path." St. Joseph was one of the humble and little persons of the world. He did nothing great in the eyes of men. He was a simple village carpenter, yet we have only to spend a day with him to learn how to keep interior recollection amid all the distractions and cares of the world, for all he did was done for and with Jesus and Mary. He earned their daily bread by hard labor. He toiled in his little shop, he was hired by others, he suffered when work was slack or when his employers were unjust, but he kept his deep interior peace because of his continual, loving cooperation with Jesus and Mary.

If we also spent the whole day entirely for God and with Jesus and Mary, if our work, our play, our conversations were all done as though Jesus and Mary were present, which indeed they are, we too would become deeply interior souls. We would be less likely to complain. We would be ashamed to lose our temper or let ourselves become engulfed in self-pity. Our burdens would be less heavy and we would find a spirit of peace and contentment permeating our lives and the lives of those about us, for wherever we were, there, too, would be Jesus and Mary.

Colloquy

"St. Joseph, how much I love you! How much good it does me to think of your humble, simple life. Like us, you lived by faith. Everything in your life was just as it is in ours."

(St. Thérèse of the Child Jesus)

Jesus, Mary, Joseph, may my last words be:
Jesus, Mary, Joseph!

⚘⚘⚘ MARY OUR MOTHER ⚘⚘⚘
"Mary is more Mother than Queen."
(St. Thérèse of the Child Jesus)

We must never forget that Our Lady, the Queen of Heaven and earth, "exalted above the stars," is a mother to each and every one of us, loving us far more than any earthly mother could love her child. There is even an additional motive for her love, as I belong to her special Order of Carmel of which she is Patroness and Mother. A mother's duty is to train her child for life, and a good mother does this with deep love and a firm hand, not giving in to her child's every whim and desire. I must remember that in the same way Our Lady watches over me and trains me for eternal life. She loves me unutterably, with a strong, efficacious love, not a weak and sentimental love. When I am beset with trials and difficulties she does not always make things easy for me — she loves me too much! She knows that they come from the hand of her Son, and that they are good for me, training me for eternity, preventing me from straying off the path to Heaven. Although she does not always lift the cross, she will inevitably give me courage and strength to face up to whatever her Son asks of me. I shall have unwavering confidence in her, and with St. Thérèse say, "Only the Immaculate Virgin presents herself in absolute purity before God's Majesty. Since she loves us and knows our weakness, what have we to fear?"

Colloquy

"But, good Blessed Virgin, it seems to me that I am more fortunate than you, for I have you for my Mother and you have no Blessed Virgin to love. Jesus on the Cross gave you to us for our Mother, so we are richer than you, since we possess Jesus, and you are ours as well."

(St. Thérèse of the Child Jesus)

❧❧❧ THE VISITATION ❦❦❦

"When I read in the Gospel that Mary went with all haste into the hill country of Judea to fulfill her duty of charity to her cousin Elizabeth, I see her pass by on her way, so beautiful, so calm, so majestic . . . . Her prayer, like her Son's, was always 'Ecce!' Here I am."

(Bl. Elizabeth of the Trinity)

After the Annunciation, Mary rose in haste and made her way across the Galilean countryside. She was full of grace as the angel Gabriel had declared, and therefore her overflowing love of God was expressed in her abounding love for her neighbor, in this case, her aging cousin Elizabeth. She did not wait to be asked to help, but went voluntarily to offer her services.

We so often think there is nothing we can do to help. We say, "I wish I could help, but what can I do?" We should always remember that every little bit helps. It may be by a helping hand here and there at the expense of our own moments of leisure, or by a kind word. Who knows, but that it may just be the kind word or act that some discouraged person needed to set him back on his feet again. More than that, it may be the very word that gives some soul the strength to resist a temptation or turns a straying sheep back to God. There are many lonely persons whose day we can make bright by the warmth of our charity. No, we must never think that we can do nothing to help others, rather, we must beg Our Lord to so fill our souls with His grace that the scales will fall from our eyes and we will see the immense amount of good that even the least of us can do for His "little ones."

Colloquy

"O faithful Virgin, when you uttered your 'Fiat', the greatest of all mysteries was accomplished in you. In what peace and recollection did you live and act! Teach me to sanctify my most trivial actions and to spend myself for others when charity requires it, yet all the while to remain, like you, the constant adorer of God within me."

(Bl. Elizabeth of the Trinity)

✐✐✐ BETHLEHEM ✐✐✐

"Is it really demanding too much to make room in our life for our Savior, so that He may transform our life into His own?"

(St. Teresa Benedicta of the Cross [Edith Stein])

"There was no room for them at the inn." In Bethlehem, Christ's own city, where it had been foretold by the Holy Spirit through the prophets that the Messiah would be born, there would be no room. "No room," is all the answer Joseph receives when he knocks on each door. Some are keeping their rooms for the rich who can pay well; some are rude; some are insulting; perhaps there are some who are a little sorry; but the answer is always the same: "No room." Why did they miss such an opportunity to welcome the Son of God? Why do we miss such opportunities? Why do we keep our hearts crowded with thoughts that keep the Christ Child out? Are we so busy with worldly plans and desires and even sins that there is no room for the Holy Family?

One man was found in Bethlehem who was willing to provide at least a stable. Let us do more and open wide our hearts in loving reparation, begging the Christ Child to enter and stay with us "even to the end of time." Let us look into our hearts and find out what is taking up the room that Our Lord wants for Himself.

Colloquy

"O Prince of Peace, to all who receive You, You bring light and peace. Help me to live in daily contact with You, listening to the words You have spoken and obeying them. O Divine Child, I place my hands in Yours; I shall follow You. O let Your divine life flow into me."

(St. Teresa Benedicta of the Cross)

THE MAGI

"For each of us a Star is shining in the heaven of our souls, pointing out the place where we shall find Jesus."
(Mother Aloysius of the Blessed Sacrament)

"We have seen His star in the East and have come to worship Him." This time the Child in the manger announces His coming not by the song of His angels but by a star. The Wise Men saw the star. They knew it meant the coming of the Messiah foretold by the prophets, and they set out immediately, full of faith and courage, undaunted by the difficulties that lay ahead.

God often puts a star in the heaven of our souls. These are His inspirations drawing us ever closer to Himself. We feel in our hearts that it is His light and we have the choice of following it generously, promptly, and with great faith, or of closing our eyes and pretending not to see it. If we follow the star it will lead us infallibly to Jesus. The way may be hard. The star may seem to disappear as it did from the Magi's sight. St. Teresa suffered from great aridity for many years. St. Thérèse went through a night of seeming loss of faith, and we, too, sooner or later, must face a starless night with only the memory of God's inspiration to guide us. In this darkness, we, too, must live by pure faith until, in God's good time, the star will shine again and with the Magi we will "rejoice exceedingly" and entering in with them we will find the Child with His Mother, Mary.

Colloquy

"O my Guiding Star, the fair light of faith enlightens me to see You. What does it matter if I feel or do not feel, if I am in light or darkness, if I enjoy or do not enjoy? Only let me so fix my gaze on You, that I may never wander from Your light."

(Bl. Elizabeth of the Trinity)

～～ ST. JOHN THE BAPTIST ～～

"How glad I am to admit that others are better than I, and how ashamed I am in God's presence."

(St. Teresa of Jesus)

St. John the Baptist is a little-appreciated figure, yet he was a great celebrity of his day. Whole towns turned out to hear him preach. The rich and the poor alike came from great distances to ask his advice, yet how different was his attitude from that of most celebrities. He never tried to draw people to himself. On the contrary, he constantly pointed away from himself to "the Lamb of God." When the crowds turned from him to follow Jesus, he rejoiced as "the friend of the Bridegroom" — it was his disciples who became jealous and complained.

Am I like St. John the Baptist or like his small-minded disciples? When I meet with success or am taken notice of, how do I act? Do I grow talkative, eager to speak of my abilities? Do I always try to get most of the praise, or do I make certain that those who helped me receive their share? When I do not succeed and others do, am I the first to compliment them or do I become jealous and sulk? Above all, do I realize that the only real success is sanctity?

Colloquy

"O Jesus, I no longer care what people think of me. Truly I do not understand this pride. I believe that true heroism consists in constant fidelity to the humble and hidden way. I am happy when lost in the rank and file, and when I feel that I am counted as nothing. Then, only, can I walk in a glory that lights the soul without burning it."

(General de Sonis, OCDS)

THE SOWER

"Jesus will reveal Himself to you in proportion to the desire you have of seeing Him." *(St. Teresa of Jesus)*

When Our Lord comes to us in Holy Communion, He is like the sower in the Gospels and our hearts are like the ground upon which His seeds of grace fall. Each time I receive Him, is my heart well prepared so that His grace will bring forth fruit a hundredfold? Or will His seed fall by the wayside while I am busy following the paths of the world?

Will it fall upon rocky ground where it will spring up for a short time and then wither away when I find out that I have to give up something I particularly like, in order to correspond to His grace? Or will it fall among thorns and be choked by my love of pleasure and convenience? If I meditated more frequently on the great mystery of the Holy Eucharist and the loving patience with which Our Lord awaits my coming, I would be more fervent in my preparation to receive Him. Many of the Saints divided the time between their Communions into thanksgiving and then preparation for their next reception. If only we had their love for this "gift of God", we, too, would be more careful to prepare our hearts for the great graces He longs to give.

Colloquy

"O my Lord, though in so many places men leave You alone or treat You wrongly, yet You endure all this and will continue to endure it for the sake of finding but one single soul who will receive You with love. Let me be that soul. Live in me and give me life." *(St. Teresa of Jesus)*

❧❧❧ CALMING THE TEMPEST ❧❧❧

"I count on Him. Suffering may go to its limit, but I am sure He will never abandon me."

(St. Thérèse of the Child Jesus)

"And behold, there arose a great storm on the sea, so that the boat was covered by the waves; but He was asleep." After a long, hard day of preaching, Our Lord was so tired that He slept through the violent storm: He, the omnipotent God, the Strength of our weakness, slept seemingly unaware of the danger. Terrified by the crashing of the tempest, the disciples rushed to awaken Him, begging Him to save them. He did so, but was disappointed in their lack of faith which had caused such fear. They believed enough to call on Him for help, but they did not believe that although He slept, He still watched over them.

How often in our own souls the storm rages and Jesus seems to sleep. Let us call on Him for help; it may be that He will calm the tempest, but if He continues to sleep and we do not feel His help, then we must believe that He is asking us to be men and women of deep faith. It is such a privilege that He should trust us so much! Let us trust Him in return. We believe in God's unutterable love for us and in His infinite power. We know that He is with us in all the tempests of life and will never forsake us. "Behold, I am with you always . . . ."

Colloquy

"O my Lord, how true a friend You are, and how powerful! For You, to will is to do, and never do You cease to love! . . . You give, O Lord, severe trials to those who love You, but only that in the excess of their trials they may learn the greater excess of Your love. Let all men rise up against me, let all created things persecute me, let the devils torment me; but You, Lord, do not fail me: for I have already experienced the benefits which come to him who trusts only in You!" *(St. Teresa of Jesus)*

⨯ THE MULTIPLICATION OF THE LOAVES ⨯

"So pleased is God with the hope in which the soul is ever looking unto Him, that it may be truly said of it that it obtains all it hopes for." *(St. John of the Cross)*

When Our Lord questioned Philip, "Whence shall we buy bread that these may eat?", He was asking of Philip a splendid act of faith, for the Gospel continues, "this He said to try him, for He Himself knew what He would do." We know what followed — Philip calculated how much would be needed to feed the five thousand and realized it would be an impossibility. He did not know what to do. We, too, often find ourselves in perplexing situations and we anxiously try to resolve our problems. That is good; we must try, just as Philip did. But Philip did not go far enough: he stopped at his human calculations instead of turning to Our Lord and saying, "Lord, I do not know how to feed them, but You are all-powerful, and You know what to do." Our Lord, Who is vitally interested in each of us, understands our problems, and He knows what to do about them. Let us then always turn to Him — He is the all-knowing, all-loving One. If we have faith in His power to help, and if we do what lies in our own power, then we can be at peace and know that in some way He will bring all things right in the end.

Colloquy

"O Lord, how often have I sought for help from other people and had more confidence in worldly aids than in You. Now I see clearly that You alone are a true Friend, and will never fail me. I firmly believe that You can do whatever You will. Grant me Your grace both in the present and in the future." *(St. Teresa of Jesus)*

❧❧❧ THE BLIND MAN ☙☙☙

"What do the great of the world matter to me if I have no desire to please them, should I by so doing cause the least displeasure to God." *(St. Teresa of Jesus)*

"A certain blind man was sitting by the wayside, begging." Poor, blind, unwanted, despised, yet in his misery he had greater wisdom than the learned Pharisees, for he asked the one question necessary and asked it of the right person: "Lord, that I may see." We, too, are beggars at life's wayside and it is only too easy for us to become so involved in the struggle for material success that we become blind to the things that are God's. Every day in some way or other we are faced with choosing between Christ's way and the way of the world. Sometimes the wrong choices are obvious and as good Christians we promptly turn them down, but there are so many small temptations that are so much a part of our daily surroundings, that we accept them as almost necessary "because everyone else does it", and we are afraid of what people will say if we are "different."

We are very blind when self-interest is involved, and we need badly that light of truth which only Christ can give us. If we humbly acknowledge this and each morning pray for this divine light, Our Lord will open our eyes, and we will see clearly to choose only the things that are pleasing to Him.

Colloquy

"O my Lord, when we see that You protect us from dangers into which we rush, how can anyone believe that You will not save us when our only aim is to please You? I can never believe it. Eternal Father, 'Lead us not into temptation but deliver us from evil. Amen!' " *(St. Teresa of Jesus)*

❧❧❧ THE BARREN FIG TREE ❧❧❧

"When, in the morning, we feel no courage or strength for the practice of virtue, it is really a grace: it is time to rely on Jesus alone."

(St. Thérèse of the Child Jesus)

It is hard to understand Our Lord's cursing of the barren fig tree, unless we realize that it is a parable in action. We are the fig tree and Our Lord comes to us expecting to find fruit, and finds only leaves. He comes to us so often during the day and we do not recognize Him — He is in that unpleasant situation, in that irritating neighbor, and He is also in that unexpected joy, and in the monotony of everyday work. He is coming, looking for real faith, for courage, for love, and so often He finds just leaves — we had promised Him all sorts of things and had made such good resolutions — but nothing came of them, no fruits were produced and Our Lord goes away disappointed. Let us beg Him, the Divine Gardener, to send rain down upon our fig tree, the rain of an abiding sorrow for our sins and for having caused Him pain. This sorrow will bring forth the fruits Our Lord loves best: humility and confidence, and little by little more and more fruits will appear, and Our Lord's loving hunger for our souls will be satisfied.

Colloquy

"O Jesus, I know well that You do not look so much at the greatness of my actions, as at the love with which I do them. It is true I am not always faithful, but I shall not lose courage. I desire to make use of every opportunity to please You."

(St. Thérèse of the Child Jesus)

THE AGONY IN THE GARDEN

"It is for us to console Our Lord, and not for Him to be always consoling us."

(St. Thérèse of the Child Jesus)

Loneliness is one of the hardest trials to bear. We are so alone. We long for a comforting word and there is no one to whom we may turn. It is then that we can faintly begin to understand Our Lord's sorrowful complaint to His sleeping disciples during His Agony in the Garden — "Could you not, then, watch one hour with Me?" He, too, longed for human consolation and would receive none, not even from those who loved Him so much. He would drink His chalice utterly alone.

St. Teresa had a special devotion to the mysteries of Our Lord's life in which He was most lonely, because she could show her love by comforting Him, and every night before going to sleep she would think of Our Lord in the Garden and try to console Him with her love. Can we not also do the same and watch one hour with our beloved Master, forgetting our own griefs in order to comfort Him for all the sufferings that our sins have caused Him? He so longs for our sympathy and love. Then, as we kneel by Him, we will find that our own sorrows have been lessened and that in return for our comfort, He has given us "the peace of God which surpasses all understanding."

Colloquy

"Are you reduced to such sore straits, my Lord, that You are willing to consort with such a miserable companion as myself? Yet Your look tells me that You find some comfort even in me. Of what have I to complain? Your labors and sorrows were so much greater than mine. Let me only comfort You."　　　　　*(St. Teresa of Jesus)*

◢◢◢ PETER'S DENIAL ◤◤◤

"I can well understand how poor St. Peter fell. Poor St. Peter! He relied on self instead of leaning on the power of God."　　　*(St. Thérèse of the Child Jesus)*

The story of Peter's denial is a sad one and makes us sorrowful every time we meditate upon it, whether we think of Jesus' side of the question or of the disciple's. Peter, newly raised to the priesthood, a few hours after his First Communion, the rock upon which Christ had promised that His Church would be built, has denied his Master three times. No one can doubt the disciple's intense love for Jesus, but still, out of fear of human respect, he has denied Him. Jesus has heard those denials and has turned, and with eyes full of pitying love, looked upon Peter. How often have I felt the same loving look when I have been unfaithful! How have I reacted? Have I tried to forget that look, or, like St. Peter and the other repentant Saints, have I let that look work on my soul? Peter, instantly filled with remorse, going out, began to weep. St. Teresa, though she never sinned seriously, always bewailed her early faults and tepidity. Do I? Or, after having confessed the same sins many times, going out, do I forget all about it and return at once to the same occasion of sin?

Colloquy

"O my God, how truly do You need all the love You have for Your creatures, to bear with us so long! How often we fail to make the effort to overcome a very small thing or to flee some occasion of sin. O true Strength, I firmly resolve to die a thousand deaths rather than offend You again." *(St. Teresa of Jesus)*

❧❧ THE CARRYING OF THE CROSS ❦❦

"I cannot think of anything more pleasing to God than assisting His suffering members."
(St. Teresa Margaret of the Sacred Heart)

Jesus fell while carrying the cross under the weight of His suffering and exhaustion of body, and no one helped Him rise. He who had been compassion itself to the weary and sorrowful, found no one in the crowd who would come forward. Let us help Him by helping His creatures. We meet with many who are struggling to rise after a fall, sometimes after years of serious sin, and are trying to make their lives over again. They meet with so little sympathy and so much scorn. Let us see Christ in them and strive to lift Him by lifting them. Perhaps there were some on that Good Friday who would have liked to help but did not dare to do so because of human respect. They were afraid of what people might say. When we see one of Christ's little ones struggling to live down the past, let us be filled with Christ's own compassion and put out a helping hand. We can be certain that in doing so we have lightened the weight of our Master's cross. Never let us look down on them. Condemn the sin, but never the sinner. God alone is judge. Let us ask Our Lord to fill our hearts with His own compassion for our fellow-men.

Colloquy

"O my Jesus, how deep is Your love for the children of men! The greatest service we can render You is loving and aiding them. Then do we possess You most entirely. Who loves not his brothers loves not You, O Lord, for Your Blood, shed for us, bears witness to Your boundless love for the sons of Adam." *(St. Teresa of Jesus)*

THE PRECIOUS BLOOD

"Look not on our blindness, my God, but on the streams of Blood shed by Your Son for us."
(St. Teresa of Jesus)

One drop of Our Lord's Precious Blood would have been sufficient to cleanse the whole world from sin and to redeem us all. Yet Our Lord was not content with one drop. He would not be content until in His infinite love for us He had actually poured out the last drop from His Sacred Heart on the centurion's spear. Yes, His Blood stained the grass of Gethsemane, the soldier's scourges, the floor of the praetorium, the streets of Jerusalem. "Why so much, O Lord?", we are tempted to cry out. Why such a waste when one drop would have been sufficient? Is that not the cry of a selfish heart, a niggardly soul? Why? Because love never counts the cost. Love must give all.

We measure our gifts, count our sacrifices, just keep the Ten Commandments so as to save our souls. Dear Lord, why am I not more generous? Why do I, again and again, offer myself entirely to You each morning and then throughout the day cut off a little here and there? By the merits of Your own Precious Blood, give me the grace to no longer count the cost, but to give all.

Colloquy

"O my God! How You have suffered for us who grieve so little for Your pains! You have shed all Your Blood for us. O what can I do for You? Strengthen my soul, and then, my Jesus, ordain the means whereby I may do something for You. Let me not come before You with hands so empty."

(St. Teresa of Jesus)

THE BURIAL OF JESUS

"If you wish to be a Saint, it is not hard. Have one aim: to please Jesus and to unite yourself more intimately with Him."   (St. Thérèse of the Child Jesus)

The terrible day of Good Friday was over and the small group took the body of their beloved Master to the tomb. The hands that had healed lepers, opened the eyes of the blind, hands always raised in blessing, were crossed in death. The feet that had walked the streets and paths of Galilee so many times on errands of love and mercy, were still. The lips that had comforted and pardoned so many were silent. A life of utter goodness had ended and all those who had loved Him and felt His kindness knew that something beautiful had gone out of their lives.

What will be the thoughts of those among whom we have moved, when we are gone? What will have been the effect of our lives on theirs? Let us hope and pray that when our bodies are laid in the tomb, that they may be the bodies of Saints: Saints who have eased the burdens in others' lives and made them happier and better, Saints who have been the living proof of the beauty and attractiveness of Christian virtue, and so have brought many souls to Christ, Saints who have so faithfully imitated Christ that all our actions have been full of His love, His forgiveness and His tender compassion.

Colloquy

"O my Jesus, since You would never put unrealizable desires into my heart, I know that in spite of my littleness I can aspire to sanctity. Come, take possession of my faculties in such a way that everything I do, from being merely human and personal, may be wholly divine. I long to prove my love in countless ways, to tread in Your footsteps."

(St. Thérèse of the Child Jesus)

❧❧❧ THE RESURRECTION ❧❧❧

"If you are happy, look upon your Risen Lord, and the very thought of how He rose from the sepulcher will gladden you." *(St. Teresa of Jesus)*

He has risen as He said, Alleluia! We rejoice for His sake Who has triumphed over death, and we have reason to be glad for our own sakes, too. It is our privilege as Christians to follow Christ and He has won for us the grace to conquer our sins and to rise above selfish, earthly things. Let us generously correspond to this grace and firmly resolve always to be loyal to His love. With humble confidence may we ever "rejoice and be glad in Him." How much cause we Christians have for joy, and what tremendous need there is in the world today for joyful hearts which glory in Christ's love for them. Even in times of hardship and trial they know how to look above and beyond, and find consolation in the faith and hope of our own resurrection from the dead. Thus we shall imitate our Savior's risen life by radiating His peace and joy to those about us. Perhaps our example will draw others to rise above the empty, deceptive pleasures of this world, to enjoy true happiness in serving God with humble and grateful hearts.

Colloquy

"O my God, may all things on earth not suffice to make me cease delighting in You. I rejoice in the greatness of Your love for me and shall ever strive to repay it. May I ever say with truth, 'My soul magnifies and praises the Lord.' "

(St. Teresa of Jesus)

CHRIST, OUR FRIEND

"All things fail, but You, O Lord of all, never fail those who trust in You."   *(St. Teresa of Jesus)*

What closer friendship can there be than that between Our Lord and my soul? He is my true Friend — my sins and my unfaithfulness do not turn Him away. He loves me with a true, strong and loyal love which nothing can hinder. He understands my every problem, and has felt my every anguish. He will never fail me; He is with me always. Let me turn to Him in all my joys, in all my sorrows, in all my needs, remembering St. Teresa's words: "It is a great matter for us to have Our Lord before us as man while we are living and in the flesh. When we have many things to do, when we are persecuted and in trouble, when we cannot have much rest, and when we have our seasons of dryness, Christ is our best Friend; for we regard Him as man, and behold Him faint and in trouble.

He is our companion. With so good a Friend and Captain ever present, Himself the first to suffer, everything can be borne. He helps, He strengthens, He never fails, He is the true Friend."

Colloquy

"Blessed is he who loves You in truth and has You always at his side. What more do we need than to have at our side so good a Friend who will never leave us? O my Lord, my mercy and my good, what more do I want in this life than to be so near You that there is no division between You and me? In such company, what can become difficult? What can one not undertake for You, with You so near? Never, with Your help and favor, will I turn my back on You. "   *(St. Teresa of Jesus)*

✺✺✺ THE HEART OF JESUS ✺✺✺

"My God, I wish to enclose myself now and forever in Your most loving Heart as in a desert, to live there in You, with You, and for You, a hidden life of love and sacrifice."   (St. Teresa Margaret of the Sacred Heart)

The Sacred Heart of Jesus is our only sure refuge in all the storms of life. In every temptation we must fly to this shelter and seek strength. There and there alone is the sure and lasting safety for the weak and mercy for the sinner. No matter how fierce the tempest, He will save us from shipwreck.

We have but to take refuge in His Heart and we will have nothing to fear. He Himself said: "Come to Me, all you who labor and are burdened, and I will give you rest."

Where are we to go to find that comfort and refreshment if not to His own Heart? It is there that our tears will be wiped away when we mourn. It is there that our fears will be quieted. It is there that we will find strength to bear bitter disappointments, humiliations and injustices. It is there that we will find refreshment in the noonday heat of life when we are worn out with struggles and disillusionments. But above all, it is there that we shall find that infinite and unchanging love for which every soul consciously or unconsciously craves. O Jesus, Your Heart indeed is our only sure refuge. You Who loved us even to the death of the cross, let us abide in Your love now and forever.

Colloquy

"O Sacred Heart of Jesus, I trust in Your infinite mercy. I desire nothing other than what You wish and I give myself to You completely. Permit me to live always in Your love. In all things I shall be content if only I may take refuge in Your Heart now and in eternity."

(St. Teresa Margaret of the Sacred Heart)

CHRIST THE KING

"You, my God, are an Eternal King, and Yours is no borrowed Kingdom."   (St. Teresa of Jesus)

"All power is given to Me in Heaven and on earth." Jesus Christ is the Sovereign King of the Universe. As Pope Pius XI tells us, Christ possesses that power first by reason of His own nature and essence, and second by right of conquest. As God, He is Creator and Ruler of all creation, the beginning and the end of all things. As man, He has delivered us from the power of the devil by His Passion, Death, and Resurrection, and has made us members of His Kingdom. We are therefore entirely His, having been bought at the price of His Precious Blood. Let us try to remember always how much we have cost Him, and how much we owe Him.

To reverence Him as our King, we must be submissive to Him. Because of His mercy and His love, He, the King of all creation, came down from His royal throne in Heaven in order to win us to Himself. He became one of us, to feel with us all our joys and sorrows, our trials and fears. "He became like to us in all things, save sin." Yet He remained King, in the crib, on the cross, infinitely loving, giving Himself completely, even to His terrible Passion and Death. Let us not resist His loving rule over us. Let us give ourselves entirely to Him that

He may reign over us completely, in our minds, our hearts, and our wills.

Colloquy

"O my Lord and my King! If one could but picture Your majesty! Although You are God, I can talk with You as a friend, for You are not like those whom we call lords on earth, all of whose power rests on authority conferred on them by others. Your Kingdom, O Lord of glory and King of Kings, is without end. Your majesty is so great that You need neither guard nor escort to convince us that You are King!" *(St. Teresa of Jesus)*

◁◁◁ GOD THE FATHER ▷▷▷
"It is so sweet to call the good God, Father."
(St. Thérèse of the Child Jesus)

Our Lord's first recorded words were that He must be about His Father's business, and His last cry on the Cross was, "Father, into Your hands I commend my spirit." God, the Eternal Father, is also our Father and cares for us, His children, with an infinite love that can will only our good. "For God so loved the world that He gave His only begotten Son . . . ." Can we ever forget that? Yet, when our prayers are not answered in the way we want, or we are faced with heavy trials and bitter disappointments, do we trust our heavenly Father and see His love behind the cross? Or do we rebel and become bitter even to the point of doubting His very existence? "Even though He slay me, yet will I trust Him," was St. Thérèse's answer when tormented with doubts against faith.

He is our Father — let us love Him. He is all-wise — let us trust Him. His one desire for us is that we be with Him for all eternity — let us place our lives entirely in His hands.

Colloquy

"O Son of God and Lord of mine! You give us in Your Father's name all that can be given . . . . You ask Him to make us His children and Your word cannot fail . . . . O compassionate Father, how little do we trust You, yet You entrusted to us Your Son Himself. Blessed may You be forever, Lord, who so loves to give that naught can stay Your hand!"

(St. Teresa of Jesus)

♠♠♠ THE SANCTIFIER ♠♠♠

"The Holy Spirit is the real guide of souls: He never ceases to take care of them and never neglects any means by which they may profit and draw near unto God as quickly as possible and in the best way."

(St. John of the Cross)

The mission of the Holy Spirit is to make us saints. He is the Sanctifier, the One Who makes us holy. On the day of His first coming in the Upper Room, He transformed the bewildered and frightened apostles into souls inflamed with a courageous and enlightened love of Christ. They no longer huddled behind locked doors but went forth spreading their Master's Gospel and rejoiced when they were made to suffer for His sake. So, too, the Holy Spirit will transform us if we will only listen to Him and correspond to His inspirations. He will never force our wills for He is the Spirit of love and wants our loving cooperation. We must yield ourselves freely to His divine action and then He will prepare our souls for the supernatural life by pouring forth His grace upon us. He will permeate our spiritual life from its very beginning on the Way of Perfection by giving us light to overcome our faults and to practice virtue, but we must be very attentive to His voice. Then, little by little, if only we will let him, He will take full possession of our souls. He will inflame our hearts and enlighten our minds until He, at last, brings us to the summit of Mount Carmel, where our union with God in love will be complete.

Colloquy

"O Holy Spirit, I consecrate myself entirely to You; take me, possess me wholly. Be the penetrating light which illumines my intellect, the gentle Inspirer Who attracts and directs my will. Complete in me your work of sanctification and love.

Come, Holy Spirit, come!"

(Sr. Carmela of the Holy Spirit)

❧❧❧ THE MYSTICAL BODY ☙☙☙

"The least act of pure love is of more value to the Church than all other works together."

(St. John of the Cross)

What a tremendous privilege it is to be a member of Christ's Mystical Body, the Church, and what a serious responsibility! As the Spirit of Jesus dwells in each of us, we are so closely united that "if one member suffers anything, all the members suffer with it; or if one member glories, all the members rejoice with it." I am bound more closely to our Holy Father the Pope, down to the least member of the Church, than by the bond of any natural or family relationship. My good actions will help the Church, and my bad actions will wound her. Checking a hasty word, being kind and cheerful when I feel the contrary, may be the means of obtaining renewed courage for some poor, persecuted priest at the end of his strength. St. Teresa founded St. Joseph's in Avila so that "being all of us employed in interceding for the Champions of the Church . . . we might to the utmost aid this Lord of mine." As a member of the Secular Order of Discalced Carmelites, I must be inspired by the same zeal, offering my prayers, my daily tasks, my sufferings, for the Vicar of Christ, the persecuted Church, and for all the members of the great Body of Christ.

Colloquy

"My God, I love You! I love my Mother the Church, but how shall I show my love since love proves itself by deeds? I can neither preach the Gospel nor shed my blood . . . but what does it matter? I will make profit out of the smallest actions and do them all for love."

(St. Thérèse of the Child Jesus)

BAPTISM

"I see in each newly-baptized infant a creature justified, and in the Church another Child capable of giving honor to God."

(St. Nuno, Carmelite Lay Brother)

"Unless a man be born again of water and the Spirit he cannot enter the Kingdom of God." As Our Lord said these words to Nicodemus, He was speaking to the whole world, explaining that without Baptism we cannot be members of His Church nor heirs of Heaven. As most of us were baptized before we understood what it meant, it is well for us to meditate on the vital importance of this Sacrament. From Baptism flows every other grace we have ever received or will receive. At Baptism we died with Our Lord in His Passion, and we rise with Him in His Resurrection. As sinful children of Adam we have died and have been reborn as children of God, as "other Christs." Before Baptism we were alone and forsaken, homeless creatures; at Baptism, the Blessed Trinity comes to dwell in our souls and we rest secure in Their all-powerful wisdom and love. Let us thank God for this great Sacrament and try with all our hearts not only to preserve the grace of our Baptism, but also to perfect it each day by living as "other Christs" in the world.

Colloquy

"O my God, You say to the soul of each of us: 'I swore to you and I entered into a covenant with you . . . and you became Mine.' We have become Yours by Baptism and have been made partakers in the divine nature and have received a share in Your divine life. Yes, we have received the seal of the Holy Trinity."   *(Blessed Elizabeth of the Trinity)*

⊷⊷ THE SACRAMENT OF PENANCE ⊷⊷

"How rightly is confession called the Sacrament of Peace." (St. Teresa Margaret of the Sacred Heart)

After Our Lord's Passion and Death we can easily imagine the bitter sorrow and remorse of conscience which the eleven Apostles felt. They had deserted their beloved Master, they had failed Him in His hour of greatest need. Oh, how miserably they had repaid His love! Then on Easter Sunday evening, Jesus appeared in their midst, breathed His peace upon them, and instituted His Easter gift to the world, the Sacrament of Penance. Not a word of reproach for their cowardice and infidelity did He utter; all that was forgotten now. He knew how humbly they had acknowledged and repented of their fall, and His only concern now was to restore them to His friendship.

This same gentle Master waits for us in the confessional. He understands our frailty and loves us more than we love ourselves. No matter if our "sins be as scarlet", we have but to lay our burden at His feet in heartfelt contrition and we shall be made "white as snow." Oh, what great thanks I owe to You, my Lord, for this Sacrament of mercy and love. I may go in peace, confident that the past is forgiven and forgotten, and filled with grace and strength to begin a new life for You.

Colloquy

"O my Crucifix, it is when I look at you that I understand all the malice of sin. My Beloved, when the executioners pierced Your hands and feet and while You were enduring such torture upon the Cross, You saw my innumerable sins and all my unfaithfulness. How they made You suffer! My

Jesus, forgive me all the pain I have inflicted upon Your Divine Heart. Forgive me and look only upon my love." *(Blessed Elizabeth of the Trinity)*

THE HOLY SACRIFICE

"I am permitted to take part in the Mass, to be washed clean and refreshed, and to lay myself, with all my actions and sufferings, beside the Oblation on the Altar." (St. Teresa Benedicta of the Cross)

"Through Him, and with Him, and in Him, O God, Almighty Father, in the unity of the Holy Spirit, all glory and honor is Yours, for ever and ever." This is the climax of Holy Mass. It is the solemn moment when the whole Church, Christ our Lord and all His members, offers infinite adoration and praise to Almighty God, through the Sacrifice of Calvary which has just taken place at the Consecration. At this tremendous moment, let us unite ourselves with Our Lord, that our whole being may be taken up by Him and merged in His great act of adoration. Let us try, as the Church would have us do, to make the Mass the central point of our lives, offering all our trials and joys, our sorrows, our intentions, our friends and our loved ones, to our Eternal Father, through Christ, with Him and in Him. Do we often think of the infinite glory that ascends to God each day, each moment, through this perfect prayer? Amidst all the gloom of sin and evil in our world today, the Mass is the great light shining from Heaven to earth and from earth to Heaven. Let us do all in our power to add our own little light, that those who "sit in darkness and in the shadow of death" may see Christ, the Light of the world, and may come to have life in Him.

Colloquy

"I will go in unto the altar of God. It is not myself and my tiny little affairs that matter here, but the great sacrifice of atonement. I surrender myself entirely to Your divine will, O Lord. Make my heart grow greater and wider, going out of itself into the Divine Life."

(St. Teresa Benedicta of the Cross)

❧❧❧ HOLY COMMUNION ☙☙☙

"If while Jesus lived in the world, the mere touch of His garments healed the sick, who can doubt that when He is dwelling in the very center of our being He will work miracles on us, if we have a living faith in Him."

(St. Teresa of Jesus)

If we have a living faith in Him! How often did St. Teresa, St. John of the Cross, and all the saints and blesseds of Carmel, experience extraordinary graces after receiving Holy Communion: interior lights, solution of difficulties, strength against temptations, even bodily cures at times. It was because of their living and overwhelming faith in this Holy Sacrament. "As you have believed, so be it done to you." Our Lord comes to us in Communion with His Heart full of love and His hands full of graces for us. If we do not receive them it is only because we have not asked for them. It is our own tepidity, our laziness, our willful distractions, our weak faith that keeps Him from doing the work in our souls that He longs to do. Do we not hear over and over again His sorrowful cry: "Oh, you of little faith, why did you doubt?" If we do not feel an ounce of devotion, no matter. We can always kneel humbly and say: "Lord, I do believe, help my unbelief" and He will come. He only waits to be asked.

Colloquy

"O Lord of Heaven and earth, is it possible while we are still in this mortal life for us to enjoy You with such special friendship? I am quite sure that if we could but once approach the Most Holy Sacrament with great faith and love, it would suffice to make us rich. How much more so if we approach it often! If we but prepare to receive You, You never fail to give in many ways."

(St. Teresa of Jesus)

❦❦❦ CONFIRMATION ❦❦❦

"Like the Apostles I looked forward with joy for the promised Comforter, gladdened by the thought that Confirmation would make me a perfect Christian."
(St. Thérèse of the Child Jesus)

Today when atheism and immorality are rotting the whole foundation of society, it takes great courage and even heroism to remain loyal to Christ and His Church. Never before have we so desperately needed the graces of the Sacrament of Confirmation — we feel so weak and helpless before the onrush of sin and evil. Yet, because we have received this great Sacrament of strength, we are "perfect Christians", that is, the Holy Spirit has given us and continues to give us all the graces we need to live as perfect Christians. He, the Spirit of Jesus, comes to us with the fulness of His gifts, gifts which enlighten our mind to see what we should do, and which strengthen our will to do what we know is right. It is this Sacrament which makes us soldiers of Christ, not only on the defensive, ready to sacrifice even life itself in order to remain firm in our Faith, but also on the offensive, making us real apostles, inspiring us with zeal to bring the whole world back to Our Lord. Let us take courage then: we have been made strong in Christ through His all-powerful Spirit, and with Him we "can do all things."

Colloquy

"Come, O life-giving Spirit, to this poor world and renew the face of the earth, and give us Your peace, that peace which the world cannot give. Help Your Church, give her holy priests and fervent apostles. Give strength and help to those who are tempted, and light to those in darkness and in the shadow of death."

(Sr. Carmela of the Holy Spirit)

✎✎ THE ANOINTING OF THE SICK ✎✎

"If you only knew how much I am suffering! I need God's help." *(St. Thérèse of the Child Jesus)*

Christ in His great love has provided for our every need. No sooner are we born than He comes to bestow on us by Baptism the initial graces of salvation. He accompanies us all during our earthly existence through the other Sacraments and then when we need Him most, in the hour of serious illness, He is there again at our side. In the Sacrament of the Anointing of the Sick, our Divine Physician comes to comfort and strengthen our suffering bodies and lighten our heavy hearts. Sometimes Christ will bring healing with this Sacrament, but at other times it will be our preparation for our journey towards our Father's house. Let us not wait until we are at death's door to call for His priest, for then, how shall we recognize Him and benefit fully from His Presence? He is the Divine Physician of our souls as well as our bodies, and His healing power will penetrate to our very hearts and cleanse us of our sins. Then we shall be filled with His peace and, placing our hand in His, we shall go with Him to His eternal kingdom.

Colloquy

"O my God, I desire to be well again only if thereby I might serve You better. I shall try to bear my sickness with joy and leave myself entirely in Your hands. You know what is best for me."

(St. Teresa of Jesus)

❧❧❧ GOING HOME ❦❦❦

"All things pass so quickly that, if only our minds faced this truth, we would not weep for those who die and go to gaze on God, for we should rejoice in their gain."

(St. Teresa of Jesus)

It is hard to say the last good-bye to our dear ones even when we know that they have served God well. We long to keep them with us, and yet, are we not being selfish? For "eye has not seen, nor ear heard, nor has it entered into the heart of man, what things God has prepared for those who love Him." St. Teresa said that to mourn excessively for one who, freed from earthly miseries, has passed on to true life, is as though we did not believe in an eternal life. If we thought more often of the life that is to come, we would indeed forget our grief and instead rejoice that another soul had gone to be with God forever.

The Saints saw this so clearly. Blessed Elizabeth of the Trinity wrote to her family during her last illness, "Do not weep over your Elizabeth . . . . O, dearest mother, let us look on high. It rests the soul to think how Heaven is our Father's house; that there He awaits us as beloved children, who are returning home after having been absent for a time; and that in order to lead us there He becomes Himself our traveling companion. Farewell! Everything tells me that I am about to depart to my Father's house. If you only knew the serene joy with which I am awaiting that face-to-face meeting!"

Colloquy

"O my Jesus, in such a trial, only You can speak, for You are the supreme Consoler. You wept at the tomb of Lazarus, and I know that You are near me and that Your Heart is full of compassion. You have received on high, the soul so dear to me. Let me live with You in that world beyond, which is really so close, for then death cannot separate us."

(Bl. Elizabeth of the Trinity)

◈◈◈ THE COMMUNION OF SAINTS ◈◈◈
"I will spend my Heaven doing good upon earth!"
(St. Thérèse of the Child Jesus)

We so often forget that in heaven we have a host of friends who long to help and console us. There is no Saint who has not walked on life's roads. Some ran their course quickly and died young, others lived to an advanced age. Some were sinners, some never offended God. Some stayed home, some traveled far. No matter, they were once as we are now, and they understand our trials and sufferings in a way that even our best friends on earth can never do. They long to help us if only we will turn to them in our need. St. Teresa and St. John of the Cross are the spiritual parents of every Carmelite. Can we doubt that they look upon us as their children and that they watch over us with loving care? Then there is a host of others from the earliest days of our Order: St. Simon Stock; the warrior St. Nuno; the lovable laybrother, Ven. Francis of the Infant Jesus; St. Thérèse; St. Teresa Margaret. Additionally, there are those closer to our own days: St. Teresa of the Andes, the youngest of our saints; Bl. Elizabeth of the Trinity; St. Teresa Benedicta of the Cross who was killed in the Nazi gas chambers; and in our own country, Mother Aloysius. They are all our brothers and sisters. If we turn to them in our needs with child-like confidence, we will indeed experience the loving help of our heavenly family.

Colloquy

"O blessed souls dwelling in Paradise! Relieve our miseries and intercede for us with the Divine Mercy that He may give us some little share of your felicity and the certain knowledge that you possess. O Souls inflamed with love, teach us how you gained such endless bliss. Draw water for us who perish with thirst in this world!"

(St. Teresa of Jesus)

THE VOCATION OF LOVE

"Lord, I shall not allow anyone to love You more or to desire Your glory more ardently than I do."

(St. Teresa of Jesus)

The Carmelite vocation is a vocation of love. All through the teachings of St. Teresa and St. John of the Cross runs the cry, "What return of love can we make to a God Who has so loved us?" And their answer is always the same: to try in our poor, human way to imitate as closely as possible the infinite love that Jesus has for His heavenly Father and for all mankind. This should be the aim of all those who wear Our Lady's Scapular, for, as St. John says, "The smallest act of love has more value in the sight of God, is more profitable to the

Church, and to the soul itself, than all good works together." The mountain of Carmel is a mountain of love and every step we take up it should be marked with an increase in love for God and neighbor. A Carmelite nun accomplishes this by a life of solitude and silence in a strictly enclosed monastery, so that her prayers and sacrifices for the world will be more intense, while we who are members of the Secular Order of Discalced Carmelites are called to fulfill this same vocation of love in the world. The two paths may seem very different, but it is the same mountain and there is but one summit — perfect love, which is union with God.

Colloquy

"O my God, I want to work for Your glory and for that I must be wholly filled with You, and You are love. Then I shall be all-powerful. A look, a desire, will become a prayer that cannot be resisted and that can obtain everything. Apostle, Carmelite: it is all one!"   *(Blessed Elizabeth of the Trinity)*

❧❧❧ OUR HOLY SCAPULAR ❧❧❧

"Whoever dies clothed in this Scapular shall not suffer eternal fire."

(Our Lady's promise to St. Simon Stock)

The Gospel for the feast of Our Lady of Mount

Carmel is the Gospel of Calvary, where Jesus said, "Woman, behold your son . . . son, behold your Mother." From that moment, Mary became the Mother of all men and bears for each of her children a tender, maternal love. She has proved this love countless times, but Carmelites glory in having received from her a unique and precious gift which seems to designate them as her "favorite children."

The Brown Scapular is the pledge of our Mother's special care and protection, and its privileges have been sanctioned by many of the Holy Fathers. With what devotion and gratitude we should treasure it, as we strive daily to become more worthy children of such a Mother! We have dedicated our lives to her, and are under the obligation of imitating her virtues, for this is the most perfect honor we can render her. If we are faithful to her in this way, we may have complete confidence that she will always protect us during this life. In time of temptation, doubt, or trial, let us have recourse to Our Lady, venerate her Holy Scapular, and we will experience her powerful help. And then in our last hour the sweet assurance of our Mother's presence will make easy for us our journey through death to "our Father's house."

Colloquy

"Mother of Carmel, I kiss your Holy Scapular and thank you for this precious gift. Help me and guide me always. I place my confidence in your intercession. Never has it been known, dearest Lady and Mother, that anyone who fled to your protection was left unaided."   *(St. Nuno)*

⊲⊲⊲ ST. TERESA OF JESUS ⊳⊳⊳

"Holy Mother St. Teresa, look down from Heaven, and visit this vineyard and perfect that which your right hand has planted."

(Antiphon for St. Teresa's Feast)

St. Teresa of Jesus is the spiritual mother of all Carmelites, and as her children we should strive to imitate her dauntless spirit. "God gave to her a heart, wide as the sand that is on the seashore," sings the Liturgy of her feast day. Great-souled, magnanimous, ardent, she could stop at no half measures. Hers was a soul of vast desires. There was no room for anything small or petty in her outlook. To her there was only one way of serving Our Lord and that was by total self-giving. Her ideal of love was to love without measure. For her this meant a complete and joyous self-sacrifice for her divine Master's interests, for His Church, and for all souls redeemed by His Precious Blood. "Let there be nothing which we know could further Our Lord's service that we dare not undertake with the assistance of His grace . . . . Ever nourish this holy daring, for God aids the valiant!" she exclaimed.

She was Teresa of Jesus and His will was her only aim.

As members of the Secular Order of Discalced Carmelites, we must imitate her wide and generous spirit, as well as her tremendous personal love of Our Lord and His Church. We must show this love by letting His will be our only guide in all the duties of our state in life; by our great respect for His bishops and priests; by our joyful obedience to all that the Church commands, and by our deep and unwearying charity to our neighbors.

Colloquy

"He who loves You truly, Lord, has only one ambition, that of pleasing You. O Lord, grant that my love be not the product of my imagination, but be proved by works. May Your Majesty allow me to render You some service and to care for nothing save returning to You some part of all I have received." *(St. Teresa of Jesus)*

ST. JOHN OF THE CROSS

"O my Love, all for You and nothing for me!"
(St. John of the Cross)

St. John of the Cross is both the spiritual son of St. Teresa of Jesus and the spiritual father of the Discalced Carmelites. Perhaps, though, we feel a little frightened at his famous doctrine of

"Nothing, Nothing, Nothing," fearing that it means that we must strip ourselves of all that is warm and beautiful in our lives. Such an interpretation is coldly inhuman and utterly contrary to the great mystical doctor's teaching. His cry of "Nothing" comes from a heart so inflamed with love of God, of neighbor, and of all the beautiful things God has given us, that it will have nothing to do with anything that might hinder this love. "A bird tied by a string is held back just as firmly as one bound by a rope," he said. And by that "Nothing" St. John of the Cross, with a great sweep of love, would cut through every strand that keeps a soul attached to the "things of earth." St. Thérèse used this doctrine for her "Little Way", and we, too, can follow this path if we keep in our hearts nothing except love for God and neighbor, nothing except God's will as the guide for our actions, and nothing except Heaven as our eternal destination.

Colloquy

"O Jesus, when shall I be wholly inflamed with Your most sacred Love? When shall I be united to You with a love so strong that no enticement of the world, or the flesh, or even death itself, can break our union? Let nothing intervene, and take away all impediments. Let me be one with You, O my God."

(St. John of the Cross)

❧❧❧ THE SPIRIT OF ELIAS ❧❧❧

"How long do you halt between two sides? If the Lord be God, follow Him."   (St. Elias the Prophet)

"You shall love the Lord your God with your whole heart, with your whole soul, with your whole mind, and with your whole strength." This is the first and greatest of the Commandments which includes all the rest and yet, how seldom do we stop to realize what effect it should have on our daily lives! God made us to know Him, to love Him, and to serve Him, and so often our days are spent giving Him the barest minimum, while we seek for ourselves pleasure, ease, and freedom from all restraint.

Our Lord said, "You cannot serve both God and mammon." Let us then serve our Master and King with unswerving allegiance. We can prove our fidelity by generously renouncing anything in our lives that is not consistent with the Divine Will. Thus shall we truly inherit the "spirit of Elias", our Father and Founder, and his dauntless zeal for the glory of God. Our living faith will be the means of drawing others from indifference and tepidity, to serve whole-heartedly the Lord God of Hosts.

Colloquy

"O my God, all I want is to serve, even if service means suffering. I know that if I were to serve You from now to the end of the world, it would be a small thing in comparison with all You have given me. O teach me that true love does not consist in enjoying consolation but in serving You with fortitude and humility." *(St. Teresa of Jesus)*

❧❧❧ LOVE OF THE CROSS ❧❧❧
"The Cross is the heritage of Carmel."
(Bl. Elizabeth of the Trinity)

Our Lord Himself told us: "If anyone wishes to come after Me, let him deny himself, take up his cross, and follow Me." A true Carmelite accepts Our Lord's command and generously tries to put it into practice — outside of Christ, nothing! In Him, all! He alone is our Model, Whom we must ever have in mind; our every action and our every sentiment must be brought into conformity with His. We must be completely caught up into the intimate life of the Man-God who became Victim for our redemption. This is the meaning of the supreme place the cross holds in Carmelite spirituality as taught by St. Teresa and St. John of the Cross. The cross is everywhere: it points the way our Divine Model has gone, and by which we must follow if we would be with Him. "Our love is the measure of the cross we can bear," wrote St. Teresa. "Desire to make yourself in suffering somewhat like our great God, humiliated and crucified:

for life, if not an imitation of His, is worth nothing,"
said St. John of the Cross. If we would follow in
their footsteps, we, too, must claim the Cross as our
heritage.

Colloquy

"O Prince of all the earth! You are indeed my
Lord! If it be Your will to suffer thus for me, what
do I suffer for You in return? I will count all trials
that come to me as gain, that I may imitate You in
something. Let us go together, Lord; where You go,
I will go, and I will follow where You have
passed." *(St. Teresa of Jesus)*

ᴅᴏᴀᴅ FRATERNAL CHARITY ᴏᴅᴏᴅ

*"We cannot be sure if we are loving God, but we can
know quite well if we are loving our neighbor. And be
certain that the farther advanced you find you are in this,
the greater the love you will have for God."*

(St. Teresa of Jesus)

"Bear one another's burdens and so you shall
fulfill the law of Christ." We are all burdened in one
way or another, with physical or moral weakness,
heavy responsibilities, fatigue, insecurity . . . all feel
the need of help and comfort. As Christians who
belong to the Mystical Body of Christ, each of us
should help the other, our hearts being open to the
needs and interests of all. The cares and anxieties of

others are our own because we are all so closely united in Christ as to form one Body. He is the Head, we the members.

"If you love Me, keep My commandments . . . this is My commandment, that you love one another." From Our Lord's words we see that unless we love our neighbors, we cannot love God; and St. Teresa tells us that the quickest way to find out if we really love God, is to examine ourselves on our love for our neighbor. If we remember that what we do to our neighbor, we do to Christ Himself, it will be easier to show an active compassion for others, even for those we dislike. Our Lord made no distinctions of persons. The feeling of love is not necessary. The active will to love is real love.

Colloquy

"O Lord, the surest sign of my love for You is the degree of perfection with which I keep the commandment of charity toward my neighbor. If I use my best endeavors and strive after this love in every way I can, if I forego my own good in my concern for theirs, however much my nature may rebel, if I try to shoulder some trial in order to relieve my neighbor of it, You will certainly give me even more than I can desire. But I must not suppose that this will cost me nothing. Besides, Lord, did not Your love for us cost You, too? To redeem us from death, You died such a grievous death as the death of the Cross."

(St. Teresa of Jesus)

◄◄◄ HUMILITY ►►►

"The more we know ourselves, the more humble we will be. Humility is walking in truth."

(St. Teresa of Jesus)

True humility is not weakness nor is it the result of an inferiority complex. Only the strong and courageous can be truly humble. When St. Peter trusted in his own strength, he denied Our Lord through fear; when in his old age he was crucified for His Master, he embraced the cross with joy. He had learned to distrust himself and place all his confidence in God. "God resists the proud, but gives grace to the humble."

Humility is truth and if only we have the courage to accept the truth of our own nothingness and our utter dependence on God, the greater will be our confidence in Him and the more complete our distrust of self. We will have an ever deepening appreciation of the fact that we are indeed "children of the heavenly Father" and that He wants to sustain and help us every minute with His love and His grace.

As St. Teresa says, true humility, however deep it may be, neither disquiets nor disturbs the soul;

instead it is accompanied by peace, joy and tranquillity. It enlarges the soul and makes it fit to serve God better; false humility, however, only upsets the mind and troubles the soul.

Colloquy

"O Christ, our only Good, it is by setting my eyes on You that I shall learn true humility. By looking at Your purity I shall see my foulness, and by meditating on Your humility I shall see how far I am from being humble. May my understanding thus be ennobled, so this self-knowledge will not make me timorous and fearful."

(St. Teresa of Jesus)

PATIENCE

"Lord, give me greater patience, that I may be able to suffer still more for You."

(St. Teresa Margaret of the Sacred Heart)

How often we are inclined to be impatient, to act without thinking, to allow ourselves to be upset by an injury or slight, perhaps only imagined. Whenever we are perplexed as to what course to take, instead of rushing blindly into action, we should stop for a moment to regain control of ourselves and to pray for light. We must beg for the grace to know how to wait and to rest wholly on God's providence. This must be our aim as we strive to imitate the patient Son of God.

Think of the contradictions, indifference and misunderstandings He bore so meekly during His life on earth, and who can ever fathom the depths of the patience He exercises now toward the sins of mankind. We each know only too well how gently and patiently He has waited for us. This must be the measure of our patience with others. Let us then beg God for the grace to accept with resignation the things we cannot change and to bear our daily cross with the loving patience with which His only Son bore His.

Colloquy

"O my God, I shall try to prove my love for You by acting with patience and charity toward those who cause me suffering. Help me not to yield to interior bitterness, and sweeten my mind with charitable thoughts."

(St. Thérèse of the Child Jesus)

❄❄❄ FIDELITY ❄❄❄

"I believe that true heroism consists in constant fidelity to the humble and hidden way."

(General de Sonis, OCDS)

Infidelity in little things can be like termites eating the beams of a house. As long as there is no shock, the house stands; but when a shock comes, the house falls. It is the same in the spiritual life. Our Lord warned us: "He who is faithful in a very little thing is faithful also in much." If we are unfaithful and doze spiritually, one day a serious temptation will come unexpectedly and we will fall. The lives of the saints are like mosaics formed of tiny fidelities that in the end make up the total picture of sanctity. It is wrong to say, "If only I had more opportunities, I could do more." St. Thérèse led an obscure and uneventful life, yet practiced her Little Way with such perfect fidelity that at the end of her life she could say, "From the age of three, I have never refused the good God anything." Let us then be very faithful to all the small duties of our state in life for love of God. It is our certain road to great sanctity.

Colloquy

"O my Jesus, I can offer You only little things, yet how often I miss the opportunity of welcoming these small sacrifices that bring so much peace! But I shall not let myself be discouraged. Grant me the grace to be more watchful in the future, for I wish to make profit out of the smallest actions and do them all for love."   *(St. Thérèse of the Child Jesus)*

CHARITY IN SPEECH

"It came to be understood that where I was, the reputation of absent persons was safe."

(St. Teresa of Jesus)

Can I say the same thing about myself? Are other persons' reputations really safe in my hands? Do I speak of them as I would want them to speak of me, or do I readily join the ranks of detractors? Am I the kind of person who faithfully gives praise to God every morning, and then shortly afterwards verbally tears to pieces someone "made in His image and likeness"? "If anyone does not offend in word, he is a perfect man," and "Blessed are the peacemakers." But what of the talebearers, those troublemakers who break up homes, destroy friendships, and spread unhappiness wherever they go? Surely they are the "whitewashed sepulchers" of which Our Lord speaks, rattling with the bones of their neighbors' dead reputations. How severely our gentle Savior condemned them.

How welcome, on the contrary, are those who are kind of tongue. They see no evil, they hear no evil, they speak no evil, and like their Divine Master, they pass through the world radiating goodness and consolation. O my Jesus, You Who are so blind to my faults, grant me the grace to be blind to the faults of others and to defend the absent as I would want them to defend me. If the actions of my neighbors have a hundred facets, let me see only the best one.

Colloquy

"O my Lord, grant me the grace to understand what it is to love You and my neighbor, that I may never speak ill in the slightest degree whatever of anyone. Let me keep most carefully in mind that I ought not assent to, nor say of another, anything I should not like to have said of myself."

(St. Teresa of Jesus)

TRUE FORGIVENESS

"In order to profit from injuries, it is well to reflect that God has been offended by them before I have, and if He bears with the injury, why should I resent it?"

(St. Teresa of Jesus)

Daily we beg God to forgive us our trespasses and we confidently trust in His mercy. Yet are we equally merciful to others? Do we really forgive *and* forget? Or do we become irritated and sulk, and refuse to speak to someone who (at least so we imagine) has deliberately hurt us? Our merciful Jesus is so kind and forbearing to us. He never reproached St. Mary Magdalen for her past life of sin, nor has He ever reproached us, no matter how frequent our falls or how often we have wounded

His Sacred Heart. We know we need His mercy so much and are so grateful to receive it. We have heard His words, "Father, forgive them, for they do not know what they are doing." Why then are we who are trying to imitate Our Lord, so slow to forgive and forget? The next time we are tempted to bear resentment against our neighbor, let us first pause to count the number of times Jesus has forgiven us, and then remember that one day we, too, will stand in need of a merciful judgment and eternal forgiveness.

Colloquy

" 'Forgive us our trespasses as we forgive those who trespass against us.' Accept my wish to pardon others, O my God, for I believe that I could forgive my neighbor anything, since You pardon me. Your Son must forgive me, for no one has done me any real injustice; therefore, I have nothing to pardon." *(St. Teresa of Jesus)*

❧❧❧ OBEDIENCE ❧❧❧

"The highest perfection consists in bringing our wills so closely into conformity with the will of God that, as soon as we realize He wills anything, we desire it ourselves with all our might." *(St. Teresa of Jesus)*

"What manner of man is this, for the winds and the seas obey Him?" Our Lord as God is absolute

Ruler of the universe. He it is "that sends forth light and it goes, and calls it and it obeys Him with trembling." All His creatures, except the noblest of them, obey His sovereign will. Only man, made in His image and likeness, refuses obedience, and disrupts the harmony of creation. What a terrifying thing is our free will! We can disobey our Creator, our Lord, our Master. He commands us through the Church, through those who are over us, and through our conscience, yet we can decide to pay no attention to His voice. Let us join with all creation, praising Him through our obedience, not only as His creatures, entirely dependent on Him, but also as loving children of a merciful Father. Let us instill this great ideal of obedience into our children, remembering that the obedience of Christ redeemed man who had lost Heaven through disobedience, and that obedience today will bring the world back to Him.

Colloquy

"O my God, reflecting that You have made me to love and serve You, I am determined to renounce my own inclinations in order to follow the way it pleases You to lead me. I shall strive always to obey. May I learn from You, my God, Who made Yourself obedient for me in far more difficult circumstances."

(St. Teresa Margaret of the Sacred Heart)

❧❧❧ HOPE ☙☙☙

"Have great hope in God and a courageous heart, for this His Majesty loves greatly."

(St. Teresa of Jesus)

All through Our Lord's predictions of His Passion runs the wonderful promise that after three days He will rise again. His suffering is ever before His eyes; He knows only too well the anguish and pain that await Him in His Passion, but He does not lose Himself in that feeling of dread and fear. Looking beyond, He sees His triumph over death and the glory that will come of it. In our trials and sufferings let us unite ourselves to Our Lord, not only in His agony and sorrows, but also in His vision of the future. This hope gives us immense strength. It is one of the three great theological virtues without which we cannot make progress in the spiritual life or understand Our Lord's teachings. We know with certainty that our sufferings united with Christ will bring us not only "an eternal weight of glory" in the next life, but also peace of soul in the present. Hope takes us out of ourselves, broadens our horizons so that we are not unduly occupied with our miseries, and lifts our souls to the vision of what one day will be ours forever — our Eternal Home, where God "shall wipe away all tears, where sorrow shall be no more, and where He will be our God and we shall be His people" forevermore.

Colloquy

"My soul seems to find rest, my Lord, in meditating upon the joy which it will have if by Your mercy I be granted to see You. I shall praise You forever, for You have prepared for us a Kingdom that has no end, in exchange for a few brief trials set amid a thousand joys, trials which will be over tomorrow." *(St. Teresa of Jesus)*

THE PRACTICE OF THE PRESENCE OF ⊷⊷⊷ GOD ⊶⊶⊶

"One must try continually so that all his actions may be a sort of little conversation with God; not in a studied way, but just as they happen."

(Brother Lawrence of the Resurrection)

The humble Carmelite, Brother Lawrence of the Resurrection, is little known, and yet he has traced a very simple way to union with God by constant fidelity to the Practice of the Presence of God. He cultivated this awareness of God's Presence in his heart so carefully that at last he could say, "The time of action does not differ at all from the time of prayer. I possess God as tranquilly in the bustle of the kitchen as if I were on my knees before the Blessed Sacrament." His smallest actions were done for love and all during his work he continued to speak familiarly with God by offering up to Him all his services and begging His graces. We, too, can follow this simple and direct way to union with God by remembering His Presence within us and speaking lovingly and humbly to Him. A hundred times a day, wherever we may be, we can turn to Him in loving conversation, asking for His help and advice in the little needs of the day as they occur. We know that He hears us. There is no need for formal prayers — He is our dearest Friend.

Colloquy

"My God, I believe that You are really present in my heart and see all that passes and will pass within me and in all creatures. What can I fear when I am with You? Do with me as You please, for I wish for nothing but Yourself and to be all Yours."

(Brother Lawrence of the Resurrection)

✍✍✍ BECOMING OTHER CHRISTS ✍✍✍

"O my Christ, immerse me in Yourself; possess me wholly; substitute Yourself for me, that my life may be but a radiance of Your life."

(Bl. Elizabeth of the Trinity)

"He must increase, and I must decrease." This is our life's work, we emptying ourselves of self, and Christ filling the void until we become other Christs. Yet, we cannot do this by ourselves. Our

Lord Himself does it by means of events and persons in our daily life. Sometimes the means are bitterly painful, but provided room is being made for Christ, what does it matter? Disappointments, uncongenial surroundings, seeming injustices, separations, painful remarks, inconsiderateness, loneliness, and a thousand other things, are the instruments He uses to empty our hearts so that He may utterly fill them with Himself. Self may try to rebel at times, but the more Christ increases in us, the less we will be concerned about self. Our outlook will be more loving and kind and we will see more and more the beauty in those around us.

Let us not shrink back, then, before the prospect, but beg Our Lord to increase in us, whatever the cost. Let us beg Him to take such complete possession of us, that His goodness will shine through us, so that those with whom we come in contact may see and be eager to follow Him.

Colloquy

"I give myself completely to You, my only Love, so that You alone can work in me according to Your plan. My God, I desire nothing, save to become Your perfect image; and since Yours was a hidden life of humiliation, love and sacrifice, so also I wish mine to be."

(St. Teresa Margaret of the Sacred Heart)

⚘⚘⚘ OUR STATE IN LIFE ⚘⚘⚘

"Let us first do our duty, and leave the rest in the Hands of God."

(*General de Sonis, OCDS*)

Our Lord as Head of the Mystical Body, in His infinite wisdom, has placed each of us in a certain state of life: laborer, business man, doctor, housewife, office worker — married or single, no matter. We each have our own small place and Jesus has given us all the talents necessary to achieve sanctity in and through the duties of that state. Perhaps we are sometimes tempted to be discontented and to feel that we could make more spiritual progress or be of more use to the Church in some other state of life . . . if only I had more time to pray like so-and-so . . . if only I had more opportunities to take part in religious activities . . . . But no, our duties as husband, father, wife, mother, breadwinner, come first. Of course we must fulfill our religious obligations to the best of our ability; then, if we have time for extras, let us use it joyfully, but never to the detriment of our other duties. Many pious persons do not realize this and as a result, their work, home, or family life suffers, and Our Lord is not pleased. For thirty years He faithfully performed the hidden duties of family life. He has set us the example; let us imitate Him.

Colloquy

"O my God, I believe that there is some good to be done around me by reason of my position. How unworthy an instrument You have chosen! Yet, I shall try to accomplish the work of Your providence to the best of my ability."

(General de Sonis, OCDS)

❧❧❧ OUR DAILY TASK ☙☙☙

"I am in deep peace — in the heaven of the Divine Will."

(St. Teresa Benedicta of the Cross)

When we awake in the morning, the duties and cares of the day at once begin to press upon us. We feel inclined to rush out and throw ourselves into them. But no! The first act of the day belongs to God in the offering of myself into His Hands. Then, I will set about whatever work He gives me for the day, and He will give me the power to accomplish it.

When fatigue, unexpected interruptions, or annoyances during the day, rob our soul of its morning freshness, then we must get to know where and how to regain our peace. This can only be found in God, in the peaceful haven of His holy will. A few moments of silence, alone, to recollect that He is really there with us, and to ask His help in our efforts to please Him, will strengthen and encourage us.

When night comes, and a backward glance shows unfinished work and much that we are ashamed of, then we must take it all, just as it is, lay it in God's Hands, and leave it in His keeping. We have tried our best and Our Heavenly Father will accept our offering and bless us with the grace to start afresh the next day, "like beginning a new life".

Colloquy

"O my God, fill my soul with holy joy, courage and strength to serve You. Enkindle Your love in me and then walk with me along the next stretch of the road before me. I do not see very far ahead, but when I have arrived where the horizon now closes down, a new prospect will open up before me and I shall meet it with peace."

(St. Teresa Benedicta of the Cross)

✶✶✶ OUR GOOD EXAMPLE ✶✶✶

"Each one of us ought to act as though the perfection of the Church depended on our personal conduct."
(St. Thérèse of the Child Jesus)

These days, we hear so much about ecumenism and how to make the Catholic Faith understood and appreciated by non-Catholics, but in the end we are Our Lord's best message, and the example of good Christian lives will draw more souls to Him than any number of dialogues. We are His hands and His feet and His lips. What does it matter what we "say" about our religion, if our actions belie our words? What if our feet are not following His pathways, but going after dubious pleasures? What if we follow the latest extreme fashions in clothes instead of dressing with Christian modesty? What if the jokes to which we listen and the books we read are sometimes shady? What if our business deals are not quite open and aboveboard? What if we scorn another's race or religion?

As Carmelites, it is our vocation to bear witness to Christ and our love of His Blessed Mother. Our Lord told us to let our light shine forth before men. We should so live that our belief in the teachings of our Catholic faith shows plainly in all our words and actions. Then, indeed, we can be certain that Our Lord's message will be clear to all the world.

Colloquy

"O my God, I ask You to make us genuine in our love, that is, men and women of sacrifice. It is our mission to prepare the ways of the Lord by our union with Him. In contact with Him our souls will become like a flame of love, spreading through all the members of the Body of Christ which is the Church." *(Bl. Elizabeth of the Trinity)*

❧❧❧ RECREATION ☙☙☙
"Lord, deliver us from gloomy saints!"

(*St. Teresa of Jesus*)

As Our Lord shares our sorrows, so does He share our joys, large and small, and He is as much with us during our hours of legitimate pleasure and recreation as He is during our spiritual exercises. All good things come from His hand and He only waits to be asked to put His blessing on everything He possibly can. He performed His first miracle of changing the water into wine, to save a young couple from embarrassment and to make their wedding party happier, and can we doubt that He smiled at and blessed their pleasure? Could we imagine the Holy Family remaining shut up in their little home at Nazareth, absorbed in prayer during some innocent village festival, or that they did not have their own small gatherings of family and friends now and then? Surely, they must have been the most warm-hearted and friendliest of neighbors.

We must ask Our Lord and Our Lady to join us in all our pleasures and recreations. As they went to the marriage at Cana, so will they come to us. Nor do they ever come empty-handed, but always bring a blessing of peace and joy.

Colloquy

"O Jesus, if our sorrows belong to You, so do our joys. Teach us not to become absorbed in selfish happiness, but to accept gratefully the small pleasures You sow in our life's path, uniting them to Your joys while on earth for the salvation of souls."   *(St. Thérèse of the Child Jesus)*

❧❧❧ FAMILY AFFECTIONS ❦❦❦
"I cannot understand saints who did not love their families."   *(St. Thérèse of the Child Jesus)*

Never has there been a heart more full of warm, human love for family and home than the Heart of Jesus. How He must have grieved over the death of St. Joseph! What tender care He took of His Mother! Yet, too often, people think that Christian detachment means that we must strip ourselves of all family affections. Far from it. God means us to have them as a part of His all-embracing plan of Divine Love for us, and they are a great grace and blessing. We must not try to suppress or limit these family affections, but only to keep them well-ordered and always directed by and united to our love of the Eternal Father. By giving us endless opportunities for self-sacrifice and self-discipline, our family affections become a source of great sanctification both for ourselves and those we love. It is only when we let these affections become selfish and irresponsible that they harm our spiritual life and make us and those around us miserable, because we are then using them for our own consolation and self-satisfaction rather than for God's glory and our loved ones' eternal good.

Colloquy

"O my God, I ask You for myself and for those whom I hold dear, the grace to fulfill Your holy will, and to accept for love of You the joys and sorrows of this passing life, so that we may one day be united together in Heaven for all eternity."

(St. Thérèse of the Child Jesus)

❧❧❧ DAILY TRIALS ❧❧❧

"I propose to have no other purpose in all my activities, whether interior or exterior, than the motive of love alone." (St. Teresa Margaret of the Sacred Heart)

If I want my interior life to grow, I must remember that every event of each day is given to me as an opportunity of growing in grace and drawing closer to Jesus. In times of temptation, Jesus is present, asking me to grasp this chance of imitating Him more closely by following His counsels. Am I tempted to impatience fifty times a day? "Learn from Me, for I am meek and humble of heart." To pride? "Blessed are the poor in spirit, for theirs is the Kingdom of Heaven." To unkindness? "As long as you did it for one of these, My least brethren, you did it for Me."

All tiresome interruptions and difficulties and stupidities, far from being obstacles to the deepening of my interior life, are instead golden opportunities to attain a greater union with Our Lord. Always so patient, He is only waiting for my cooperation with grace to draw me closer to His Sacred Heart. If, when faced with these daily trials, I withdraw into the center of my soul where He is waiting for me, and draw strength from Him to resist these temptations, then one day I shall be able to say with St. Paul, "It is now no longer I that live, but Christ lives in me."

Colloquy

"My God, since You are with me and since I must occupy my mind with these external things, I beg You to grant me the grace to remain with You and to keep You company; but that it may be the better done, my Lord, work with me, receive my labors and possess all my affections."

(Brother Lawrence of the Resurrection)

❧❧❧ DISCOURAGEMENT ❦❦❦

"God deliver us from saying, when we fall into any imperfection, 'We are not saints!' Although we are not, with the aid of God, we can be if we strive our hardest."

(St. Teresa of Jesus)

We all suffer from periods of discouragement in the spiritual life. It is often because, like the Apostles, we feel that we have toiled all night and taken nothing. We know that we have tried our best; we have struggled with this or that fault or weakness day after day, sometimes for years, and still our nets are empty and all we can see are failures. It is then that we are tempted to give up and be content with mediocrity. "I was never meant to be a saint," we tell ourselves defensively, which is exactly what the devil wants us to say. Discouragement is one of his best weapons because it undermines our trust in Our Lord. If only we would realize that there can be no real failure, no matter what the externals may show, if we just place our whole trust in Him, ask for His help, and then patiently continue in our struggle. He is watching, He is near us, His love surrounds us. At the moment He knows to be best for us, He will speak the word and our nets will indeed be filled with a miraculous catch.

Colloquy

"O my God, You see how easily I lose heart at the thought of my imperfections. Nevertheless, I shall continue to strive after virtue. Gladly will I forego all consolation in order to offer You the fruit of all my efforts. I wish to make profit out of the smallest actions and to do them all for love."

(St. Thérèse of the Child Jesus)

❧❧❧ TEMPTATIONS ❧❧❧

"It is here that love must be made known, not in secret places, but in the midst of temptations."

(St. Teresa of Jesus)

Temptation holds a vital place in our spiritual life, because without it there would be no merit, nor any way to prove to God that we love Him more than ourselves. "Because you were acceptable to God, it was necessary that temptation should prove you." Temptation ranges from mere annoyance to real agony, and Our Lord, in order to help us, subjected Himself to diabolical temptation. In that struggle with Satan, all of us were beside Him and He won for each of us the victory over our temptations. Let us have absolute confidence in Him, and let us meditate often on Psalm 90, "You who dwell in the shelter of the Most High," knowing that no matter how violent the temptation is, God will never let us be tempted beyond our strength. When we are greatly tempted, how miserable we feel, and how far from God we seem to be, even after resisting heroically! Is that perhaps an echo of Our Lord's Agony in the Garden? In any event, no matter how badly we may feel, we know by faith that we are stronger, purer, and holier than ever before, and Our Lord says to us in the depths of our hearts, "Well done, good and faithful servant."

Colloquy
"O Eternal Father, what can we do save to have recourse to You and beg You not to permit our enemies to lead us into temptation? O my God, never must we cease to beg Your help. Give us, O our good Master, some safeguard in this most dangerous warfare."

(St. Teresa of Jesus)

⊲⊲⊲ THE DEVIL ⊳⊳⊳

"The soul cannot overcome the devil without prayer, nor penetrate his devices without humility and mortification."

(St. John of the Cross)

Today, most people scoff at anyone who really believes in the devil – such a ridiculous figure, depicted with cloven hoof and forked tail! Actually, they would be right if that were the kind of devil we believed in. Do we ourselves realize who the devil is? The Church teaches us that Satan was once Lucifer, the Light Bearer, the magnificent archangel whose beauty, power and intelligence surpassed any other created being. We cannot begin to fathom the splendor that was his. After his rebellion, he was cursed by His Creator, and became the Prince of Darkness, but lost nothing of his tremendous power or intelligence.

Thinking men and women today can see him at work in our world, yet how clever he is to masquerade as a harmless imp! He is the great adversary of mankind. He would turn the world upside down to snatch a single soul from God. But let us not fear, he is weak as an infant as long as we are humble and trust in Our Lord, Who protects us under the shadow of His wings, Who is our refuge and our stronghold.

Colloquy

"O my God and my true strength! How is it, Lord, that we are so blind as to use what You give us for serving the devil? Grant that I may nevermore repay Your great love for me by loving him who hates You and will hate You forever."

(St. Teresa of Jesus)

⊰⊰⊰ **PRAYING BACKWARDS** ⊱⊱⊱

"We can never have too much confidence in the good God: He is so mighty and so merciful. As we hope in Him, so shall we receive."

(St. Thérèse of the Child Jesus)

There is no such thing as time in God's sight. Time is only for us to use as a path to eternity. For God there is no past or future; all persons and events are before His eyes this present moment and every moment. Christ, as we know, was comforted during His Passion by the love and reparation of all the faithful throughout the ages. This thought should be a great consolation to us, especially when we are worried about the salvation of a loved one. Was that soul prepared for death? Did I pray enough? Did I sacrifice enough? "If only I had done more," we say to ourselves anxiously, over and over again. Instead of grieving as one who has no hope, we should realize that there is still time to pray, and that there will be time as long as we live.

Let us trust then in God's eternal mercy, and pray and sacrifice as though that loved one were still on earth. No matter how great our love for that soul, God's love is infinitely greater. He sees our tears, He hears our prayers, and He will judge with a just but loving judgment.

Colloquy

"O my God, from the bottom of my heart I beg You to finish Your work of mercy. I have asked it often and will ask it again. I ask it, penetrated with the thought that Jesus Who has triumphed over death has also caused to triumph the soul for whom I grieve."

(General de Sonis, OCDS)

THE MEASURE OF OUR LOVE

"Our Lord does not so much consider the greatness of our works as the love with which we do them."

(St. Teresa of Jesus)

So often when we look back over our lives, we feel that we have accomplished so little for Our Lord. Others have built churches, schools, written books, or even given years of their lives to the missions, while our state of life and responsibilities keep us tied down to a humdrum existence while we long to do great deeds for our Blessed Savior. Yet all He asks is that we abide in His love.

"At the evening of life we shall be judged by love," said St. John of the Cross. That is the only measuring stick that Our Lord will ever use when we stand before His throne. How much have we loved Him and how much have we loved our neighbor? The helpless invalid, patiently going the way of the cross; the busy housewife, united to Him in her daily tasks; the working man who does his work cheerfully for the love of God: all can transform their smallest actions by love into deeds that are great in God's sight. If we fail to be saints, we have no one except ourselves to blame.

Colloquy

"O Lord and Love of mine! If You come to me, why should I doubt that I can do much to serve You? Henceforth, Lord, I desire to forget self, to seek only how to work for You, and to have no other will than Yours. But alas, I have no strength! You are all-powerful, O my God! All that I can give You is my firm resolve to serve You by my actions."   *(St. Teresa of Jesus)*

CHILD OF THE CHURCH

"I thank You, my God, that I die a daughter of the Church."   *(St. Teresa of Jesus' dying words)*

Do I really know what a tremendous blessing it is to belong to the Catholic Church, or do I more or less take it for granted? It should be a cause of immense gratitude to God — do I ever thank Him for it? He, the Creator of the whole human race, has chosen me out of millions, to be His adopted child, a member of His Son's Mystical Body. The Blessed Trinity dwells within me; Christ Our Lord Himself comes into my heart at each Holy Communion; He washes my soul in His Precious Blood in the Sacrament of Reconciliation; He has given His Mother to me to be my Mother. Have I ever thanked Him for going through so much anguish and suffering in order to give me these gifts? Those outside the Church have none of these blessings — why has He chosen me? It is through no merit on my part, but solely out of love on His part. Meditating on these graces often, will fill me with gratitude and love, and also with shame for having made Him so little return. "What return shall I make to the Lord for all that He has given me?" Let us imitate the example of our Holy Mother St. Teresa, and resolve to live in such a way that we may be able to draw others to share in the great blessings that our Lord wishes to bestow on all mankind through His Holy Catholic Church.

Colloquy

"Ah, Lord of Heaven and earth, is it then possible during this mortal life to enjoy such close friendship with You? Blessed may You be, O Lord, for nothing is wanting on Your part! I ask then, O Lord, no more of You in this life, except that even if I wished, I could not separate myself from union and friendship with You."

(St. Teresa of Jesus)

NOTES AND INSPIRATIONS

NOTES AND INSPIRATIONS

❧❧❧ NOTES AND INSPIRATIONS ❧❧❧

NOTES AND INSPIRATIONS

NOTES AND INSPIRATIONS

NOTES AND INSPIRATIONS

Made in the USA
Monee, IL
18 January 2024